S0-CFQ-780

COLORful Magic!

by Danny Orleans and John Railing
Professional Magicians

Scholastic Inc.

New York Toronto London Auckland Sydney Mexico City New Delhi Hong Kong Buenos Aires

The Color-Changing Shoelace was invented by Harold Sterling.
The authors wish to thank David Ginn and Tom McCormick for permission to include it in the Colorful Magic kit.

The authors also thank Dale Purves of Duke University and R. Beau Lotto
of University College London for permission to use their Rubik's Cube Illusion (on page 21).

ISBN 0-439-80342-X
Copyright © 2006 by Scholastic Inc.

Design: Mark Neely and Michaela Zanzani
Studio photography: James Levin
Hair and makeup: Kathy Morano

Other photo credits:
Page 21: Dr. Dale Purves and Dr. R. Beau Lotto (www.purveslab.net)

Illustrations, pages 29–31: Yancey Labat

All rights reserved. Published by Scholastic Inc.
No part of this publication may be reproduced, stored in a retrieval system, or transmitted in any form or by any means,
electronic, mechanical, photocopying, recording, or otherwise, without the prior written permission of the publisher.

For information regarding permission, write to Scholastic Inc., Attention: Permissions Department, 557 Broadway, New York, NY 10012.
SCHOLASTIC, THE ULTIMATE MAGIC CLUB, and associated logos are trademarks and/or registered trademarks of Scholastic Inc.

12 11 10 9 8 7 6 5 4 3 2 1   6 7 8 9 0/1
Printed in China
First printing, February 2006

Table of Contents

★ = easy magic trick   ★ = more challenging trick

Color Me ✦ ✦ Magic!

CrisTiaN
AmY
MaX
SoFie
Mpho
(pronounced EM–po)
Alvaro
LeaH

What happens when you make a yellow shoelace turn green? Or when you turn a red-and-blue scarf into a yellow-and-green one by sliding it through your hand? You get lots of wide-eyed looks, that's what!

In *Colorful Magic*, you'll find all sorts of great tricks with color—tricks where you'll change colors, predict colors, and even make colorful props appear and vanish! You'll...

✶ make blue-spotted cards become red—**or purple, yellow, and green!**

✶ change the color **(and flavor!) of a piece of candy.**

✶ guess which crayon **your friend picked from a box.**

✶ **create the illusion that you're** stretching a rainbow.

And plenty more! With all the colorful tricks you'll be performing with this Ultimate Magic kit, you'll put on a real eye-popping show!

Watch the Colorful Magic on DVD!

Each trick is explained with step-by-step instructions here in this book. But be sure to pop in your DVD to see the tricks demonstrated by the Ultimate Magic Club magicians on the left. That'll give you a chance to see how to present the tricks to your friends and family. Have fun making up your own jokes and stories to go along with each trick. Your magic will be much more "colorful" when you add your own style and sense of humor!

The ULTIMATE
Magic Club

COLORfUL
Magic!

©2005 Scholastic Inc.

What's in Your MaGic Kit?*

RAINBOW ILLUSION

See these two rainbows? The blue-and-green rainbow looks bigger than the red-and-orange one, doesn't it? But really, it's just an illusion—the two rainbows are actually the same size. You can use this illusion to make it seem like you're stretching paper rainbows! Check out pages 6-7 to learn the secret!

COLOR-CHANGING SHOELACE SET

With this tricky set of laces, you can make a yellow shoelace turn into a green one just by sliding it through your hand. And *then*, when your friends ask where the yellow lace went, you can pull your regular yellow lace from your pocket! That'll *definitely* leave 'em baffled. Turn to page 16 to start learning shoelace magic!

Regular yellow shoelace

Changes from yellow to green!

COLOR-CHANGING SCARF

Why does this blue-and-red scarf have a little yellow corner poking out? Because when you pull on that corner, the scarf will become yellow and green! It's a really fun trick that's a snap to learn. Flip to page 8 to get started!

MAGIC DOT CARDS

See how some of these cards have two-colored dots? That's the secret that'll allow you to turn a set of red cards into blue ones—or better yet, into a *rainbow* of different colors! Find out how to do two great tricks with these cards on pages 12-15.

Stretch a Rainbow

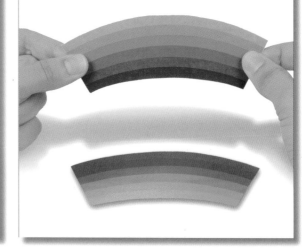

First, the red-and-orange rainbow seems bigger. Then, after you do some magic stretching, the blue-and-green one seems bigger. What's going on? Are you really changing the size of the rainbows? Nope! The rainbows are actually the same size. You're just making one *look* bigger by holding it below the other one. It's an illusion that'll really puzzle your friends!

you'll need...

⭐ **Rainbow Illusion**

make magic!

1 Hold the blue-and-green rainbow above the red-and-orange one. The blue-and-green rainbow will seem smaller because it's on top.

The illusion works best if you line up the ends like this. Then the bottom rainbow looks a lot longer!

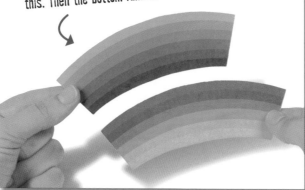

2 Put the red-and-orange rainbow down and pretend to stretch the blue-and-green one.

3 Pick up the red-and-orange rainbow and hold it above the blue-and-green one. It looks like the stretching worked!

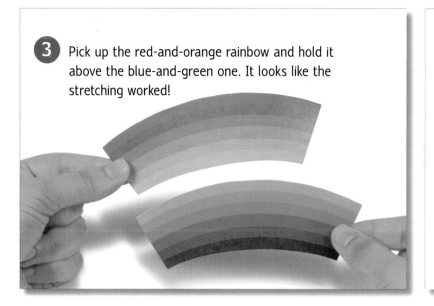

4 Cross the two rainbows, as shown below, and wave your hand over them, as if you're working a magic spell.

5 Now put the two rainbows back to back, and show your friends that they're exactly the same size, thanks to your magic!

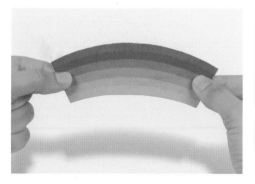
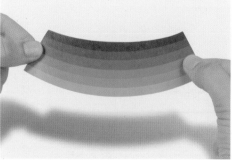

How'd it work?

The secret to this illusion is the special shape of the rainbows. Our eyes compare the long curve of the rainbow on the bottom to the short curve of the top rainbow.

Because the ends of the rainbows are cut on a special slant, we always think the bottom rainbow is bigger!

The Surprising Scarf

What happens when you pull a red-and-blue scarf through your hand? It changes to yellow and green! How's that possible? It's all thanks to the scarf's secret lining—when you turn it inside out, you get two new colors, and a hiding place for the *old* colors!

you'll need...

✳ **Color-Changing Scarf**

get ready

Pinch the scarf above the ring like this.

1 Drape the red part of the scarf over your open right hand. Then pinch the scarf above the ring with your thumb.

2 See the corner of the yellow scarf that's poking out? Wrap your fingers around it. That'll hide the secret from your friends!

1 Hold up the scarf so everyone can see both colors. Keep the yellow end hidden in your hand!

2 With your left hand, grab the ring. (Your right hand is still holding on tight to the yellow end.)

3 Close your left fist loosely around the ring with the scarf hanging below.

4 Slowly pull your hands apart. Let the scarf slip through your left hand as the ring slides down.

5 First the yellow will appear, then the green.

6 When you've pulled the scarf all the way through, hide the blue end in your left hand and show the two new colors!

Hide the blue end in your left hand.

 RESET! ★

To change the scarf back to blue and red, just grab the ring again and slide the scarf back through!

The Transformation Tube

Now that you know how to transform your scarf by sliding it through your *hand*, try sliding the scarf through a tube! When your friends watch the transformation happen, they'll think the old scarf is hiding in the tube. Then they'll *really* be surprised when you show them that the tube's totally empty!

* Color-Changing Scarf
* Cardboard toilet paper tube

get ready

1 Put the scarf in the starting position you learned on page 8 (here we've switched colors for variety). As always, hide the end that's sticking out.

Hide the blue corner in your right palm.

2 Hold the cardboard tube in your left hand, and you're all set!

1 Poke the blue corner of the scarf into the cardboard tube. Reach into the other end of the tube and grab the corner with your left hand.

Don't let anyone see the blue corner!

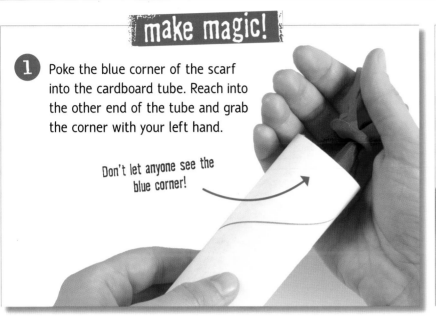

2 Turn the tube upside down and pull the blue corner through.

3 Wrap your right hand loosely around the top of the tube and the scarf's ring.

4 Hold the tube and the ring with your right hand while you pull the blue corner with your left hand.

5 When the colors have changed completely, you'll feel the ring tug on your hand. Don't let it slip through!

Don't let the ring slip out of your hand!

6 Drape the scarf over your right hand, and keep the yellow end hidden.

7 Then take the tube and tilt it toward your audience so they can see that it's empty. The green-and-yellow scarf is gone!

I've Got the Blues

Ever had the blues? It's not fun—but this trick sure is! Your Magic Dot Cards will all be blue when you hold them a special way. Then, when you replace one with a cheery red card (and secretly turn the cards upside down), the cards will all be red, and the blues will be history!

you'll need...

* Magic Dot Cards— only the red and blue ones

get ready

1 Arrange the two-color cards so the blue dots are on top. Then overlap the cards in a fan, and slide them together so no red shows between them.

The blue dots are on top.

2 Add the blue card on the right to cover the red parts on the end card. Now all the cards look completely blue!

Don't let any red show!

3 Put the all-red card in your pocket or on a table in front of you, and you're ready to chase those blues away!

12

make magic!

1 Show the fan of blue cards. Then pick up the red card and slip it between the third and fourth cards.

2 Then remove the all-blue card and set it down.

3 Close the fan of cards into a pile.

4 Now give the cards the Secret Half-Turn. To do this without looking obvious, grab the top of the cards with your free hand, and turn the cards as you change hands.

The Secret Half-Turn

  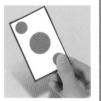

Grab the cards up here.

5 As soon as you turn the cards, wave them around as if you're working your magic!

6 Slowly and carefully spread the cards out into a fan. Make sure not to let any blue show!

Keep all the blue hidden!

Back to Blue!

To change the cards back to blue, just repeat these steps, sliding the all-blue card between the third and fourth cards.

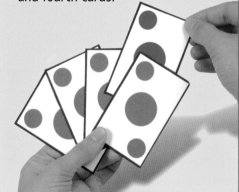

A Rainbow of Flavors

What happens when a magical blue card mixes with four red cards? You get a lot more colors! How does it work? It's the Secret Half-Turn again, just like you learned in the previous trick.

When you perform *this* trick, you can tell a story about a wizard who magically changes cherry candy into a rainbow of flavors. Check out your DVD to see how Sofie tells it!

you'll need...

* Magic Dot Cards— just the ones shown below

get ready

1 Arrange the two-color cards so the red dots are on top. Then add the all-red card on the right.

2 Close up the cards into a fan, making sure that only red is showing!

3 Put the blue card in your pocket, and you're all set.

make magic!

1 Pick up the blue card and put it in front of the red cards.

2 Close up the fan into a pile.

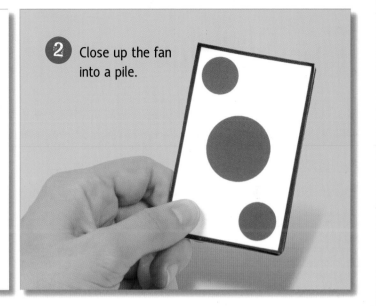

3 Give the cards the Secret Half-Turn, as shown on page 13.

The Secret Half-Turn

4 Swirl the cards in the air as you say some magic words.

5 Slowly spread the cards out, being careful not to show any red. There's your rainbow!

Keep all the red hidden!

The Shoelace Shocker!

Now that you've worked your color-changing magic on scarves and cards, it's time to move on to shoelaces! Your friends will be amazed when you turn a yellow lace into a green one just by sliding it through your hand! And when they ask where the yellow lace went, you'll pull it out of your pocket! Now *that's* a shocker!

you'll need...

* ❊ Yellow shoelace
* ❊ Color-Changing Shoelace

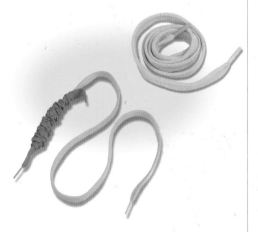

get ready

1 Put the yellow shoelace in your pocket.

2 Scrunch the green sleeve of the Color-Changing Shoelace all the way to the bottom of the yellow shoelace. To do this, hold the end of the yellow lace with one hand. With your other hand, grab the top of the green sleeve and slide it down until it's all bunched up at the bottom.

3 Put the scrunched-up green sleeve in your palm. Fold in both ends and hold them in place with your fingers.

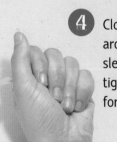

4 Close your hand around the green sleeve. Hold on tight and get ready for magic!

make magic!

1 Stretch the yellow lace between your hands to show it to your friends.

Keep the green sleeve hidden in your palm!

2 Turn your fist over and toss the lace over, too.

3 Open your pinky a little bit. With your other hand, grab the end of the green sleeve.

4 Pull on the end of the green sleeve. See the yellow lace being pulled into your hand?

5 When you can't see any more of the yellow lace, stop pulling.

6 Take the top end of the green lace with your other hand. Don't let your friends see the yellow end peeking out.

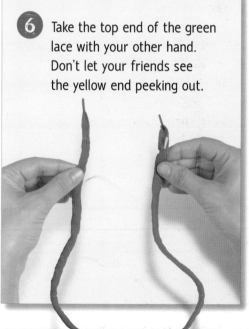

7 Where's the yellow lace? Reach into your pocket and pull it out. How did it get there? Magic!

Double Shoelace Shocker!

Want to take the shoelace trick one step further? **Then surprise your friends by hiding *another* shoelace in your hand. When they see the yellow shoelace turn green, they'll suspect that the yellow lace is really hiding in your hand! When they ask you to open your hand, you'll show them how wrong they were!**

you'll need...

* Yellow shoelace
* Color-Changing Shoelace
* Your own normal shoelace that's not yellow or green

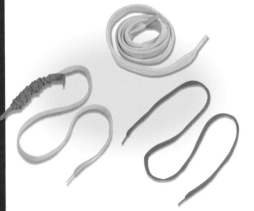

get ready

1 Do steps 1-3 on page 16.

2 Fold the normal shoelace and place it at the base of your fingers, above the Color-Changing Shoelace.

Hide the normal shoelace like this.

3 Tuck the end of the green sleeve under your pinky, and then close your fist, keeping both laces hidden inside. It's definitely a handful!

1 Change the yellow lace to green, following steps 1-5 on page 17.

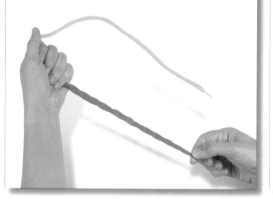

2 Then take the top end of the green lace with your free hand and hold it away from your fist. Keep your fist closed tightly!

3 Now ask your friends what happened to the yellow lace. Most likely, they'll say it's hiding in your fist! So, open your fist and let the normal lace tumble out! Surprise, surprise!

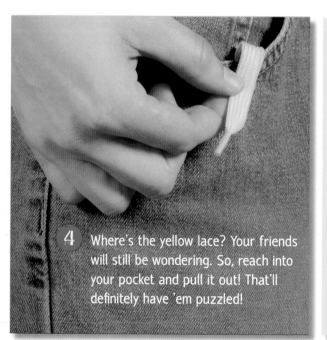

4 Where's the yellow lace? Your friends will still be wondering. So, reach into your pocket and pull it out! That'll definitely have 'em puzzled!

More Shoelace Shockers

Instead of hiding a second *shoelace* in your hand, you can sneak in other surprises! Here are some ideas:

- Make the yellow shoelace transform into a yellow ribbon!

- Hide a gummy worm in your hand and say that the worm ate the yellow shoelace!

- Hold a quarter in your hand, and say that the yellow shoelace was changed into spare change!

Color Confusion!

See the colorful cube on the right? **Can you make the brown square on top the same color as the orange square on the side? Of course you can! That's because they're actually the same color! Don't believe it? Your friends won't either, until you cover all the other colors so they can compare the two squares for themselves!**

you'll need...

* Paper
* Pencil
* Scissors

get ready

1 Make a cover by tracing the outline on the next page. You can also print the cover from **www.scholastic.com/ ultimatemagic** (look in the Magician's Bag of Tricks).

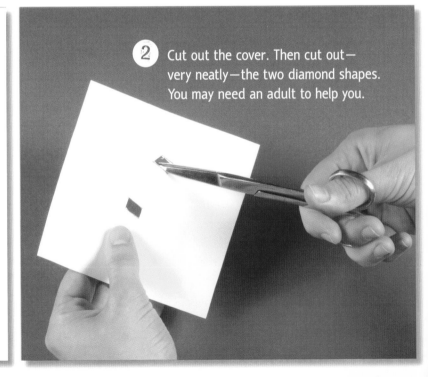

2 Cut out the cover. Then cut out— very neatly—the two diamond shapes. You may need an adult to help you.

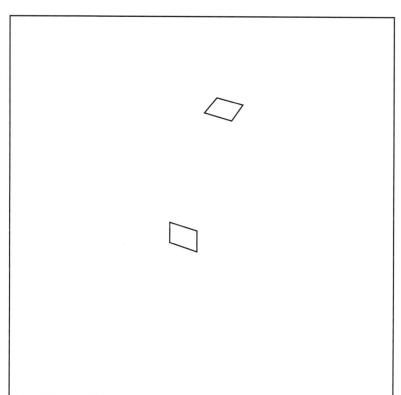

make magic!

1 Compare the brown square on the top of the cube to the orange square on the side. They look like different colors, don't they?

2 Place the cover over the cube so the two squares show through the holes. They're really the same color!

How'd it work?

The shadow over part of the cube confuses your eyes, changing the way you see the colors of the squares. When you cover up the shadow and the other colored squares, you can see that the brown and orange squares really *are* the same color!

And you know what else? The brown square below the cube, just outside the shadowed area, is also the same color as the "orange" square on the side!

My Favorite Flavor

Don't you wish you could **change any piece of candy into your favorite flavor?** Well, as a magician, you can create that illusion! Just learn how to secretly slide a candy into your lap, and you'll be able to pull off a very *sweet* trick!

you'll need...

* ⚹ **Table and chair**
* ⚹ **Two candies of different flavors and colors**

We'll use cherry candy as the favorite flavor and lime candy as the non-favorite flavor. You can use any two flavors that look very different.

get ready

1 Sit on the chair with your knees pressed together.

2 Hold your favorite-flavor candy in your left hand, pinched under your thumb. This is called the Secret Thumb Grip.

3 The other candy should be on the table where you can reach it easily with your right hand.

4 Your audience should be **facing you** so they won't see your secret move!

 tip ⚹ Watch the DVD to see how this trick will look to your audience!

Secret Thumb Grip

1 With your right hand, reach for the lime candy. Cover it with your fingers and slide it toward you.

Lime candy under here

2 When the candy reaches the edge of the table, let it fall quietly into your lap. But don't look at it!

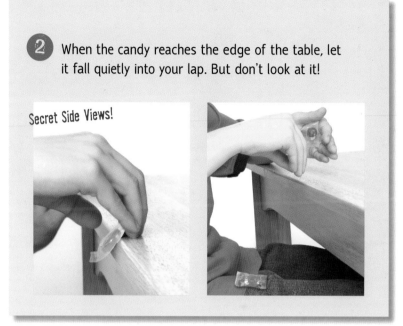

Secret Side Views!

our audience
thinks the lime
candy is here.

3 Lift your right hand off the table, pretending you picked up the candy. Keep the back of your hand toward your audience.

4 Pretend to put the candy into your left hand. Then close your left hand immediately.

5 Open your right hand to show that it's empty.

6 Wave your right hand over your left hand. Then open your left hand and show your friends that the candy's changed to your favorite flavor!

Pick a Crayon,
Any Crayon!

Can you guess the color of a crayon that's hiding behind your back? You *can* if you use the sneaky secret you'll learn in this trick! Add a touch of good acting, and you'll have your friend convinced that you can read minds!

---

you'll need...

* **Box of eight crayons**

get ready

Make sure your fingernails are clean, and you're ready to go!

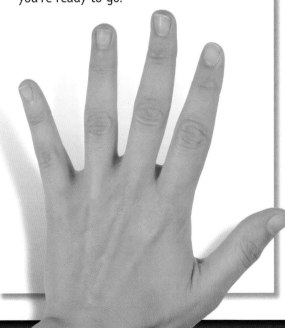

make magic!

1 Give your friend the box of crayons and turn around so you can't see her.

2 Tell your friend to pick a crayon out of the box and hand it to you behind your back.

3 Keep the crayon behind your back. Then turn around so you're facing your friend. While you're telling her to concentrate on her color, secretly scrape a little bit of the crayon with your fingernail.

This happens behind your back.

4 Hold the crayon with one hand. Bring the other hand—the one with the colored fingernail—in front of your body.

5 Hold your hand in front of your friend's forehead as if you're trying to absorb her thoughts with your hand (this is where good acting skills come in handy!). Make sure the back of your hand is facing you so you can see the wax under your fingernail.

Crayon wax is here.

6 Sneak a peek at your fingernail.

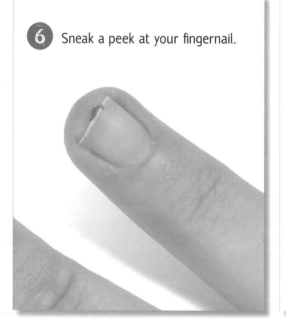

7 Then put your hand behind your back and hold the crayon with both hands again. Flick the piece of crayon wax off your fingernail.

8 Pretend to concentrate some more and then magically name the color your friend chose!

★ tip ★ Watch the DVD to see how Alvaro pretends to read his friend's mind!

25

The Vanishing Crayons

Here's another fun trick you can do with a box of crayons—but this time you'll need a box that you can turn into your own homemade magic prop. Magicians often make their own props, because they're always trying to create new tricks that no one's ever seen before. So, try making this homemade prop with a box of crayons, and see how surprised your friends are when you make those crayons disappear!

you'll need...

* Box of eight crayons
* Tape
* Glue
* Scissors
* Small cloth (like a napkin or handkerchief)
* Optional: Extra set of crayons and pencil case

get ready

1 To start, you'll need to find (or buy) a box of eight crayons that you're allowed to turn into a magic prop.

2 Have an adult cut all the crayons in half.

3 Then line up the crayons and tape them together.

4 Carefully turn the crayons over. Then drip some clear-drying glue between them.

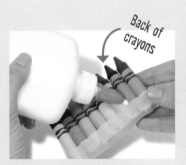

Back of crayons

5 Let the glue dry, and then put more tape on the backs of the crayons to secure them.

6 Cut the top of the crayon box to create a half-circle-shaped opening.

7 Put the crayons back in the box. The taped side of the crayons should be facing **away from you**. Squeeze the crayons so they stay at the top of the box. You're ready to make them disappear!

1 Hold the crayon box on the side, pinching the crayons so they stay at the top.

4 Set the cloth down and then grab the bottom of the box. Squeeze the crayons so they won't move. Then turn the box upside down. Your friends will think the crayons really *have* disappeared!

2 Drape the cloth over the crayon box. Then relax your grip. You'll feel the crayons slide down.

tip As you relax your grip, say some magic words (or make another sound) so no one hears the sliding crayons!

3 Then pull away the cloth. The crayons are gone!

EXTRA CREDIT

Want to add an extra surprise at the end of the trick? Here's how:

Before the trick, load a pencil case with crayons just like the ones you used to make your crayon box prop.

At the end of the trick, when your friends ask where the crayons are, dump out your pencil case to show them!

Color Predictor

When you give your friend a choice of a bunch of colors, can you really know which one he'll pick? Even before he picks it? You *can* if you know the Counting Force! It's a special counting secret that'll make your friend pick the color *you* want him to pick— even when he *thinks* he has a free choice!

you'll need...

* Color chart
* Red paper
* Hole punch
* Large paper bag
* Three or more red objects

get ready

1 Print the color chart shown below from **www.scholastic.com/ultimatemagic** (from the Magician's Bag of Tricks), or create your own version.

2 To make red confetti, use a hole punch and red paper.

3 Sprinkle the confetti into the bag.

4 Then add an assortment of red objects, like an apple, a tomato, a red marker, a red shoe, or whatever else you have available!

Sprinkle confetti into the bag, then add the red objects of your choice!

Counting Methods

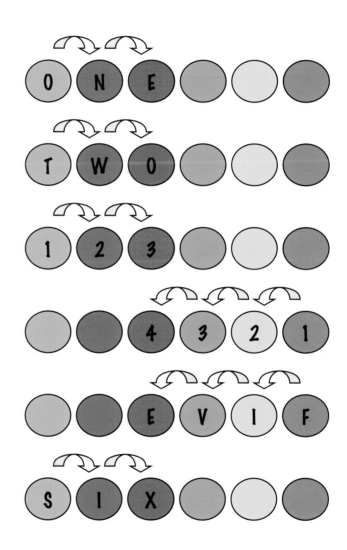

1 Show your friend the chart with six colored circles. Ask him to pick a number from one to six.

2 You're going to use the number he picks to count the circles. No matter which number he picks, you'll land on the red circle, thanks to the Counting Force. Sometimes you'll count out the number, and sometimes you'll *spell* it out.

For example, if he picks the number **one**, start on the orange circle and spell out **O-N-E**, like so:

You can see the counting method for each number on the right.

3 After you've landed on the red circle, prove to your friend that you predicted the color he was going to land on. One by one, take all the red things out of your bag. Then, as the grand finale, dump the red confetti over his head!

See You Later!

Eye Fooled You!

Here's some real color magic that works without any props. All you need is your eyes!

1 Stare at the fish's eye for thirty seconds. Try not to blink.

2 Then stare at the dot in the bowl. What do you see?

3 Now stare at the center of the purple circle on the right for thirty seconds. Then look at the center circle in the stoplight outline. What happens?

NOTE: It might help to cover the bottom half of the page with blank white paper.

4 Look for more illusions like this on the Ultimate Magic Club web site at **www.scholastic.com/ ultimatemagic** (in the Magician's Bag of Tricks)!

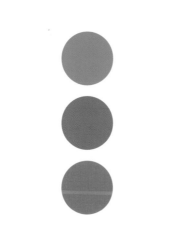

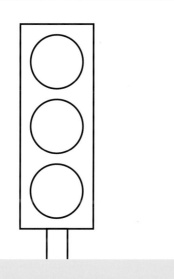

How'd it work?

After you stared at the blue fish, you saw an orange fish in the bowl, right? You should have also seen a stoplight with red, yellow, and green lights in the right places.

What you're seeing is an *after-image*, which is what happens when your eye has looked at one color for so long, the receptors for that color get tired, and the *opposite* (or "complementary") color appears.

Check out the color wheel on the right. The colors are arranged so their complementary colors are on the opposite side of the wheel. The color that's opposite blue is orange, which is why the after-image of the blue fish was orange.

You can use this color wheel to draw your own images in complementary colors, and then create your own after-image illusions!

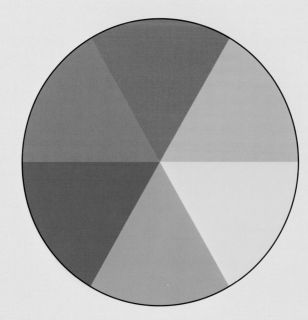

Color Wheel

Your Colorful Personality

How'd it go? Did you shock your friends with your shoelace routine? Were they amazed when your Magic Dot Cards went from red to rainbow? There's no doubt about it—colorful magic is a real treat for the eye!

Want to make your magic even better? Then watch other magicians surprise and entertain people. Watch them on video. Watch them on TV. But also try to watch them live in a theater. You'll see the many different ways that magic can be performed. Some magicians perform to music. Others tell funny jokes or stories. Each one does his or her own kind of magic—and that's what you should do when you perform your tricks. Let your colorful personality shine through!

Meet the Magicians

Danny

John

Danny Orleans

Danny is a professional magician who performs at schools, parties, and business meetings throughout North America. He got his first magic kit when he was six years old, and the first trick he ever learned was the Magic Dot Cards! When his father showed him the trick, Danny was completely fooled. Then he practiced hard to learn the trick himself. He still loves to perform it!

John Railing

John travels the world entertaining people with his magic. John's favorite colorful magic trick involves color-changing pocketknives. His black pocketknife changes from white to black and back again. Once when John did this trick, he closed his hand around the knife and told his audience to name any color. When he opened his hand, he had a handful of tiny knives in every imaginable color!